WINGS FOR MY SOUL

B. NITHEESH KUMAR

Dedicated to my beloved parents, teachers and all my dear friends.

Contents

Contents

Contents

Contents

Contents

Contents

ENGLISH QUOTES

Preface

This book contains quotes and poems that I've written and are reflections of my fluctuating emotions. I always felt relieved when I get into writing quotes and poems.

I feel that everyone have their own way of doing things and this is my way to sort things out. Just like any other poet/writer, getting my works published is a big dream for me, ever since I started writing. It feels great when I finally present this book.

We learn a lot of things through our life experiences. We learn how to behave, when where and how to show our emotions, and how to control them. We embed those lessons deep in our soul. The voice which comes from our inner side,which is sometimes consistent and sometimes not. I feel that all of my writings are a sort of life lessons to me and I embed them in my soul. Now that my soul knows those lessons, I call them as "Wings for my soul ".

Thank you,

Dr.B.Nitheesh Kumar

ENGLISH LONG FORMS

[POEMS]

1. Smile

I'm tired of greeting them,
And they know now, I'm faking my smile.
Its like hell, acting like a good boy.
Now I want to be a bad bitch !
Had much butter and sugar talk,
Let people know that I'm now diabetic.
I'm forgetting them from yesterday,
But still, they torture me in my dreams !
I fell often for love and affection,
Now, my ladders are pushing me down.
Boundaries were been laid and crossed,
But Now, nothing remained to be bounded.
My eyes hope to see my heart blooming,
They never allowed it to step out even !
Every day and every night ask me to change,
And let them out of my life for once and all.
I'm tired of greeting them,
And asking them if they're fine,
Because I was never a part of their concern.
And they know now, I'm faking my smile.
Smiles only come when heart wants to !

2. Roses and the garden

Roses want to bloom in their garden,
Whose garden welcomes flies and bees.
But, Farmer thinks love looks always beautiful.
Petals and sepals want wings and wind,
Wings grow more when love has hunger.
But, hunger sees no beauty always, to fill.
Where the roses thrive, also flies and bees ?
Wherever is their home, but they live together.
Shiny coats or filthy faces ,
Bees and flies still depend on this earth.
Unless the plant gives, seldom the bee takes,
Unless the bee gives, seldom the plant lives !
Love is for life or life is for love ?
Both are for you and you can have both !
Roses then will bloom in their garden,
Whose garden welcomes flies and bees !

3. Flower in the Barren

I'm a flower in the barren.
Don't try to hug me baby,
Coz I have thorns all over me.
If you want to stick around,
You must like me as me.
Don't try to pluck all my thorns,
I know you don't want to, and you can't !
And now you may get hurt too .
I've been thriving on much water,
Much required to breathe enough.
You've added salt and some sugar,
But that pushed back the water then.
You always wanted bushes of roses.
I'm not even able to bloom properly,
But somehow eating some sun rays.
Now that you're gone away from me,
And your scent in the wind is feeble,
I wish you could get some nice roses,
Which would fit right in your shirt pocket !

4. In a wooden canoe

I'm all alone in a wooden canoe.

In the middle of ocean, can't go anywhere.

My eyes got no shore in their field,

I want to hope, but my heart doesn't yield.

There are some fishes hitting my paddle,

And some tides that push and pull me like a cradle.

I forgot what pushed me into this mess,

But I remember,in last november

I've been scratched by a black cat to surrender !

Its hard to hope now or to give up,

But, I can hear my heart singing lub dup !

Where is my home I can't figure out now.

But, it also pretty, below the shade of rainbow.

Towards the east, said always my mother.

But, moon also shines in west, no bother !

When I close my eyes, this world is different.

My world is not true yet, but stays resilient !

Wherever I go, memories scare me.

To forget or to remember, but I let me free .

Life lies in all forms and all flavours.

Its hard to whether throw or to savour.

I'm all alone in an wooden canoe.

In the middle of ocean, can't go anywhere.

I wish to create a sweet home just here,

And make those fish friends come near !

5. Iam what Iam

Iam good, Iam bad.
Iam lazy and clumsy.
Iam stupid, Iam fat.
And ,I don't fit into your rules.
But baby, you got to know this,
I will never be your's !
When I ask you how you are,
I mean, come and hold my hands.
And, you never ask how am I ,
When you get wet by my tears,
It feels choking in my throat !
I make you happy sometimes,
And you say some evenings,
You want to spend some time with me.
When I needed your words,
You always walked away from me.
Iam emotional, Iam dumb.
Iam dramatic and incomplete
Iam messy, Iam happy !
But baby, you got to know this,
I will never be your's !
When I think of our past,
I smile and in the end, I cry.
Its hard to forget our things,

And to start new beginnings.
Every now and then, I hear your name,
In my heart and see you in my dreams.
Its just like everyone's love story,
Having no start , but an ending.
Yes, Iam mad and I'm glad.
Iam alone and Iam in streets .
Iam strong, Iam what I am !
But baby, you got to know this,
I will never be your's !

6. Lullaby

It isn't a parody.
It is a melody,
It is a lullaby.
No song that a nightingale can sing,
No scent that a night queen can bring,
Is as great as,
The love of you,
The great heart of you !
When I do listen your song,
I feel that heaven bells are rung!
So, Oh Please ! I say,
Resting on stalks of hay,
Maa ! We call,
When we played with a ball.
Please sing it deep,
So that we could sleep deep

7. My friend

Oh. My friend,
You talk about Bugatti,
Have you ever ate spaghetti?
You tell about ride of a unicorn,
Are you so rich at born ?
You whisper, murmur, you fonder ,
What a being are you, I wonder!
You talk about a royal cruise,
Are you born so loose ?
But, I say,
With proud to jay,
Having you with such a heart,
Its like to fly in a golden chariot.
However you are proud,
Having you, Iam proud !
I can say, I have got a fellow,
Like getting in campfire, a bunch of marshmallow .
Your heart is a hero,
That cruelty in you in zero.
God is great that he gave you,
It is true that I like you ..
I like you ..
I like you ..

8. All about you

I never hugged you,
I never kissed you,
So you did..
But, I feel them.
I fell for alternatives,
When you ignored me.
Didn't found that security,
In anyone's hugs..
Didn't found that sweetness,
In anyone's kisses..
That I treasured in you ,
And, In my feelings.
But, when I knew,
That we won't be together,
You aren't mine,
I felt that I'm lost !
Left for god,
That's all,
My meaningless life !

9. Everything in you

You are my shadow,
I have no nights.
You are my winter,
Your hugs make my blanket.
You are my pain,
Smiles flood my heart.
You are my hunger,
Your kisses make me to linger.
You are my morning dew,
Will not keep any of my dreams due.
You are the shoulders, my tears get rest,
My emotions never get any rust.
You never feel boring,
You are my ice cream,
Every crunch is a sweetening beam.
Your smiles are strings of violin,
Disguising love in every note.
You are my everything,
Without you, I am nothing .

10. Mother's love

Every star is a moon,
Every stone turns into a sculpture,
Every leaf blossoms as a flower,
In your love showers.
Oh my mother,
Rainbow circles out,
Tears smile even,
Dreams pile up as a castle,
Heart dances on its beat,
Holding your hands,
My wings glitter and usher,
Into the sky of deep love blues

11. Our story

You were there in my every poem,
Filled in my heart and every thought,
You cared me like someone near,
always making smiles win over fear,
I remember those eyes on your debut,
Which made you to look like an angel.
I got habituated to your sweat smell,
Stuck in your tangled hair very well.
Made my heart to trust you so much,
That drew us into this moment.
No regret, we are not together,
Yes, you'll find another person for sure,
But, you are the reason I'm grateful,
Made me know myself better than before
When I said you to be on my side,
You made it always into my tears,
You cannot just be a phase for sure,
My heart still fills its blank pages with you.
Glad that you do ask sometimes how am I ,
Yes, you'll get into another story for sure,
But, Our story might be the only one for me

12. What are we?

What do you call this place ?
I'm able to soothe my heart here,
When I close my eyes to your hum,
And feeling warmth in your lap.
Should I hug you? Or
Should I burn you in my dreams ?
What is that charm in your eyes ?
That brings smile on my lips,
And tells that I'm not alone .
Should I hold you ? Or
Should I leave you like you do ?
What is that force that connects us ?
Even we repel each other,
We know how well we are doing.
What is the relation between us ?
I'm able to see you every morning,
Even though you are miles away.
Should I ask you ? Or
Should I end the lines abrupt ?
As always, left meaningless !

13. No please

No to black please,
And a no for white too.
No to blue yeah,
And a no for pink too.
Not all in the high tones,
And not all in the lows.
My heart want to stay in between,
Or wants to stay free and all alone.
No to your melting hugs,
No to faint dainty dreams,
That'll bind you and me together,
and fake that this is forever.
No to make you the reason,
No, if you feel as victim.
No to say that our story ended,
For something that never started.
It's the same word you said,
No, if you ever remember,
The word and the writer too!

14. Old conversations

Some old conversations that
my thoughts are filled with,
and new beautiful starts
which I wish not to end,
Are merging colours in my mind.
And sky goes blue and black meanwhile.
Between circles of love and hate,
Together smiling and holding hands,
Cuckoos now are admiring crows.
Tears wet its own shoulders finally,
And smiles come from within.
Conversations now seem only as words,
But, sparks sprout from somewhere.
Hearts are connected somehow,
clinging to different rhythms,
Yet remained close as before.
Some old conversations now,
never seem to be old anymore

15. Like a good bye

Nothing remains by my side,
When I open my eyes.
At least what I dreamt,
And those memories we had,
Stay always in my heart.
Days are turning the pages,
And I know you are far away,
Too late to be on my side.
We'll never see each other,
And rarely talk about life.
I know you don't need to think,
I'll be just a name,
Somewhere in your contact list.
But can you tell my soul,
There are no crossroads.
No need to care or see,
I was never your duty.
No need to grant me any pity,
I can heal my wounds all alone.
I wish you'll not say its a phase,
and give me false hopes for living.

16. Something

Something makes a start,
Something makes an end.
Something that lies between,
Is what that makes the whole story.
Rhyming the lines remained,
Vibing to emotions vanished.
Something that was to be shown,
Something that was to be shared,
Something that protects,
Is what that builds the wall of love.
Giving smiles are now rare,
Crying hearts got killed.
Stones are made even much stronger.
Something that was meant to be,
Something that seems to be.
Stars and the sky are never together,
you know someday when you see,
Something that makes a change !

17. Wings

Let me give some wings,
to the birds which wish to fly.
Let me grow some wings,
Until my inner soul will smile,
And, is ready to explore the skies.
Invisible, they arise all from my heart,
Killing and growing love now and then.
Let me cut all my strings to earth and heaven,
They'll bleed and dry I know,
But, the heart wants them to stay alive.
Stuck on the highways of life,
And Between memories and hopes,
Made of every tear drop and my wills,
Fragile yet strong to dream and to do,
Contained or set to be liberate,
Let me give some wings to my soul,
Let me grow some wings.

18. Last friday night

Last friday night I saw,
A girl with open hair,
Staring at the stars,
In her first floor balcony.
She doesn't see my eyes,
Neither can I,
But It feels that I could,
Feel the way she feels.
Her tear drops got the shine,
And that fell into my eyes.
In a White goun, she stood
She then looked like an angel.
I went down near to her porch,
Her hairs were flowing to the wind,
And her shadow was on my side.
I hugged her silhouette,
she looked and then smiled,
Her last tear drop fell on my eyes.

19. Every time

Every time I Love someone,
I wish It should be the last time.
Every time I go to the temple,
I ask god to make me heartless.
Every time someone makes me cry,
I wish I could turn as harsh as them.
But my heart slips over emotions,
And it just wants another loving heart.
Every time I look in the mirror,
I see my insecurities reflecting on me.
Every time I see someone happy,
Sharing smiles over the internet,
I also see some jealousy in haters.
Every time I see someone coming out,
And want to live their own life,
I see barking dogs craving their blood.
Our earth is so big and beautiful,
And some can't know an inch of it.
I know, our heart is small as our fist.
But has a vast place for empathy.
Every time I see someone trying to fly,
I Wish they would reach the high sky.
Every time I get hurt by someone,
And cry sitting in a corner,

I wish it would be the last time,
Every time I Love someone,
I wish It should be the last time.

20. Catastrophe

I wish you were a dream,
Or if I could make you a statue.
I wanted it to be magical,
But it went like a catastrophe.
When I feel someone as mine,
I don't know how it happens,
And It signals them to go away.
Iam dying on the peak of pain,
No one to hear me in dark rooms,
Iam holding to the hope that I make,
Like the slightest fibre that spider makes.
I could breathe in plenty fresh air,
And feel the sun rays touching my cheeks,
But I still find me lost in the crowds,
Iam hating the people once I loved,
I need some help and some love,
Iam losing the hope on my life,
I need someone to trust and love,
And one where I could be myself.
My life is going like a catastrophe,
I wish It could be a bad dream,
I want to be beautiful and magical !

21. Flowers around us

There are flowers all around us,
Different colours, shades and scents.
No one can even pick a thorn,
But only, If we want or let them.
Morning meadows are awful,
Sunshine's and also sunsets,
If one has loving aesthetic eyes.
Butterflies and moths,
Pinks, blues, whites and blacks,
Allies and enemies are awful,
If one has loving beautiful heart.
Tears and smiles,
Pain and pleasure,
Breakups and making out in rain,
All are parts of our love stories.
If we have guts and the power,
We can hold or break the world.
Nothing is made to be called beautiful,
Everyone are equal to bleed and die,
Everyone are equal to love and cry.
There are flowers all around us,
Different colours, shades and scents,
No one can even pick a thorn,
But only, If we want or let them.

22. Our stories

Our stories were always different,
We just had a trailer in common.
I was enjoying ice creams in the rain,
And you were craving for hot desserts.
My words never had you any meaning,
And you never really thought of me,
Just the way my heart did it always.
I know that you'll forget me for sure,
I don't care about it now anyway,
But sometimes, I broke and I cried.
You tell that you know my every inch,
And understand my heart so well.
You yell that I'm obese and amenable,
And act like if you really do care,
Yes, you are gentle, and quite good,
And our worlds are actually different
We just had a trailer in common.
Our stories were always different,
Your and my stories are always different.

23. Around me

The faces around me are smiling,
And Iam still waiting for someone,
Whom I can call mine and only mine.
I don't know what it makes to love someone,
Coz I've been trying it harder,
But I've been pushed back always.
I can't find any flaws in someone I love ,
I don't know how they measure it,
And just say that we're incomplete !
Love is blind everyone say. But,
Caste and colour, all stuck their way.
Isn't it who that kill your insecurities,
Where your words don't get stucked up,
And you are loved just the way you are.
Should we make it strong with concrete,
Or just card tower falling to the winds ?
Is it the way that you make a priority,
Or just share your soul for lifetime ?
Is it only the bond between two hearts ,
Or Something involving quantum math ?
I don't know what it makes to love someone,
I don't know how they measure it,
And just say that we're incomplete !

24. Love ad libitum

This day is going to end soon,
and Iam seeing the moon in the sky,
Walking alone with my headphones,
Vibing to all tay songs all the way.
I haven't seen this world too much,
Hope you could get me there some day.
My heart is not listening to itself,
What can I do,I can't stop the hopes.
Make me a bird and I want to fly high,
But protect me in your heart cage,
Feed me your love adlibitum.
The sky looks vast and elaborate,
There's much space to be all alone,
But, you keep me sticking to your love.
The nights are dark and empty,
Still I can see some stars are shining.
You know, we got wings and all,
Let us see all the springs and heavens.
I can't control my heart, its to heavy,
Hold my hand and come sit beside me,
Say you'll never leave me all alone.
Make me a bird, I want to fly high,
Protect me in your heart cage,
Feed me your love adlibitum .

25. New me

Today I saw a new me,
Like sun came from clouds,
Like I knew everything,
The same old wily faces,
Overwhelming fake promises,
Short staying fragrances,
Which choked me in the past,
Now feel like rotten eggs,
Now, can't reach my breath.
But I can't stop screaming,
Can't urge my brain to stop,
But, sometimes, I gain control.
In a row, I know Iam all alone,
Holding my hands with someone,
When their purposes are done,
I know they'll leave me all alone.
They feel like rotten eggs,
Like I knew everything,
Today, I saw a new me

26. Hey wind!

Hey wind, bringing the smell,
You brought the memories live again.
Her hair is lying close to my fingers,
And her eyes are into my heart.
She saw something excited in my heart,
But, all went gloomy and back dim.
I know, she's out of her boundaries,
And I love her more than I do for me.
She loves that I always want her to smile,
But, I trying to smile looking at her,
There's something pulling me back,
And I can't fake it just like all the time.
She want to take me back to the roads,
We went and walked together smiling.
I know Iam out of my emotions,
And she likes me more than I do for me.
But, I can't pretend to be a shining star,
My heart is burning deep like a sun,
And I got no one's shadows on my side,
She knows that, but still cries for that guy,
I know that we are just meant to be friends,
I know, she's out of her boundaries,
And this closeness is just as I wantedHer hands are holding my fingers,
And she's trying to heal my dead heart.

Hey wind, bringing the smell,
You brought the memories live again!

27. They

They are before my eyes,
Some seem close, even they are far.
They handle my tears well,
And say Iam not alone.
I give them that priority,
Which sometimes was not their way.
I never felt so special,
As I make someone always.
They tell that they are my best friends,
But, I can't see anyone in my heart,
And my conversations seem tough.
We have different life routes,
Hearts, opinions and priorities.
But, we all want is one,
To make our friends to smile.
They tell that we are both together,
And I can call them day and night,
But I only hear their caller tune,
More than their voice over phone.
There were hours spent together,
And promises made for lifetime.
But, my heart says that it's the only one.
They are before my eyes,
Some seem close, even they are far.

They handle my tears well,
And say I am not alone

28. Hope

Somewhere beyond curly hair,
Rosy lips and white skin tone,
My heart saw you beautiful,
Straight into your kind eyes,
And you were like a small child.
I remember your warm hands,
Which hugged my heart,
And kept it tight to yours.
Then, I listened to its rhythm,
I just wanted it for lifetime.
I felt proud walking with you,
And when I was named as yours.
For the first time in my life,
Somebody felt really like mine,
Like my parents and blood line.
I kept a mirror in my mind,
And thought you feel the same.
You broke it into many pieces,
And I never fit into any places.
After many days of necrosis,
Somewhere in my rotten heart,
A seed of hope is germinating,
And I want to keep it alive !
Somewhere beyond curly hair,

Rosy lips and white skin tone,
There should lie something beautiful !

29. Ex & Expectations

I broke up with my ex and expectations,
Now, I'll handle myself, all the way I wanted.
I know that won't sound fun and calming,
I hope it would stop my heart bleeding,
Won't repeat to the same wounds killing.
He says we are friends and like brothers,
But I know, What it's meant to be a hater.
Everyone's got their circles and emotions,
But, we don't see their shadows and tears.
There's no one to praise my smile, but
There's no one to lock my steps too .
My wings will be rising from my blood,
And I finally got to know all that's mine is me.
I never used to be on someone's support,
And my feet always knew the path I was going.
The sun still rises in east for me and my hopes,
and my heart trusts me much more than ever,
I made up with my commitments and life,
Now, I'll prioritise myself in my very own life.
I broke up with my ex and expectations,
Now, I'll handle myself, all the way I wanted

30. Nobody like us

Nobody loves you more than I do,
And nobody can love me more than you,
You know, I work for you all the time,
And you point out my imperfections,
That makes my every cell feel guilty.
I'm only yours in this world you know,
And I'm what you moulded me into.
I feel dead, when you hate me sometimes,
And, its pity that we are inseparable.
You are the sculptor and you have the tools,
Design me in a healthy way,
It can be different, one in the Billions.
If you can't love me, you can't love anyone.
Look at your face and look at your hands,
See all the tears and recall all your smiles,
Aren't they worthy for having some praise?
Its you that make me and you different,
Different yet beautiful, one in the billions,
Nobody loves you more than I do,
And nobody can love me more than you!

31. Lotus

I wanted you like a lotus,
That wanted water in the pond.
I wanted you to smile forever,
Like the sun shines everyday.
I wanted you to hold my hand,
Like roots hold up the tree,
I wanted to walk along your side,
Like no one could make us separate.
But, those were yesterdays.
Now, that I know my worth,
And the value that you gave me,
Iam closing all my circles,
Drawing up the boundaries,
And I know you wouldn't care,
Like as if you cared before,
But, I miss that perfect illusion,
That said I would be in your eyes,
And I was something for you,
As You were precious to me.
I've been making things on me,
Much harder, as they grew in me,
Your love sometimes saved me.
But, those were yesterdays
Now, that I know my worth,

And the value that you gave me,
Iam closing all my circles,
Drawing up the boundaries,
And I know you wouldn't care,
Like as if you cared before.

32. Where are we?

We're growing deep into the oceans,
But can't feel tides touching our feet,
And draining our blood so sweet.
We are on that corner of the street,
Where paths to the reality got fogged,
And sheeps making their gears up,
Clogging into each other's stupidity,
We are on the edge to lose our wisdom.
We had books as fat as bread loaves,
All were pages, but not were same.
But, we still judge them by the cover,
And we never saw what was within.
The clock got tired and stuck away,
But, the time runs for all the time.
If we have brains and hearts,
That's what makes us a human,
Revert and suck all your blood back,
Feel the sunshine on your faces,
Be a butterfly and let others fly

33. Could you?

Could you see that ?
Something beyond red and fleshy ?
On its way to rot, decaying day by day,
Still not losing hope, its beating me up.
Spreading my blood infected by your love,
All-over my body and to each and every cell.
Could you feel that ?
My heart is aching, wants to meet yours.
It doesn't know that you have forgot me,
And I forgot that you never valued my heart.
Its going numb, making me a dummy doll,
It feels useless striving for a useless like me.
Could you hear that ?
Shameless, it still feels you special today,
And it can't see you suffering even little.
It wants to cut it's strings and stop you bleed,
You named it unlovable, incomplete and lame,
Still it wants to get killed to make you smile !
Could you know that ?
It loved you always the way you were,
It let your stings, go pass through it,
Feared about one sided cruel world and cried,
Thought you were that good, special one,
But, it couldn't know that you rep that world.

Its finally getting to know how to live alone,
And not to wait until someone comes,
My heart is making it on its heart ,
Could you see that ?

34. Rotten emotions

I gave you all that I could,
All of my apples jumped down,
When they knew you were hungry.
All of my branches bent down,
When your sweat needed some shade.
I felt happy when I was of some use,
And when you smiled and looked at me.
Yes, I am the seed that you have sowed,
Smaller than you, but I don't know,
The way you come and look at me,
Makes you always a small child to me.
Yes, I dried in summers sometimes,
And, I remember you were that one,
Who watered me love and nurtured.
Sometimes, you cut down my timber,
And said that I must grow a little stronger.
Now, that my bole started bleeding,
I asked you for water, and support,
You then dug my soil around
Put some tape and called me wilt,
And went around thorny rose bushes.
I gave you all that I could,
And I don't expect you to remember
All my roots and the place I've been !

35. Open your eyes

Open your eyes and have a look around,
Feed some colour to your retinas.
There are dandelions and dragon flies,
Water streams and bursting volcanoes,
Beautiful hearts and spider webs.
Life around is simple, yet diverse.
Air like magic, invisible yet gives life.
Made of cells, yet we have emotions.
Minute but sophisticated, if understood,
Everything around us is perfectly complex.
Every question may have its own answer,
Threads of some paths are yet not dragged.
Yet some don't feel secure and literate.
And wish if perfect could be a little bit more,
Than the way it is made to be perfect.
Perceive the sophisticated perfection,
Open your eyes and have a look around !

36. We

Love stays for a longer time,
Burns but turns out to be gold..
Then, ashes come in no time.
We had love and gratitude,
And we got some attitude,
We didn't leave each other till now,
And We doesn't deserve each other.
It would have been good for us,
When we wanted to exit, but
We closed each other's doors
We ran into each other's rooms,
I Smelled your bedsheet and cried,
And you made my soul feel died.
We lived without each other,
We've got no time to be together
Our hatred grew, we didn't bother,
Roots of the tree got into our nerves,
Breaking our hearts is not a new thing,
We don't deserve each other
You and me should understand
And atleast give ourselves a goodbye !

37. Sun to shine in june

Do you see the stars above are smiling ?
They shine bright when we're together.
Do you hear the ocean waves are chirping ?
They sing that our love lies in their vocals.
Do you find my heart beats much faster ?
It wants your little lips to feel the rhythm..
Do you feel that we're made for each other ?
We know that we can't stay away and alone .
Do you see the grass blades get wet, by dawn ?
They finally draw in sky, a colourful paragon.
Do you remember any worst dark nightmare?
We know we've got wings to fly and bloom,
And make the hiding sun to shine in June.
And make the hiding sun to shine in June !

38. May be I just

may be I just want you,
to sit with me sometimes,
stay closer to my soul,
get to know my heart !

May be I just want you,
to hold my hand sometimes,
Look into my eyes,
And know what you are in my dreams..

May be I just want you,
Say that you miss me sometimes,
feel the way I do it for you,
And make your watch for me..

May be I just want you,
To have a look on my appetite,
Bake me hugs and kisses,
And feed me with your hands..

May be I just want you,
To stretch your limits with me,
Break all the walls between,
Know that Iam standing for you..

May be I just want you,
To be you always,
And accept me as me
And let our story begin..

May be I just want you,
To come out of my dreams,
And grab my hand and say,
I'll keep my promises for sure.

39. Tired voices

Faking overwhelming promises,
Never coming true dreams.
The position I wanted you to be
In my life, is just what you said.
Words are wrong if they were mine,
But your side of world is always okay .
I've been again relaxing my feet,
Will you make my roses bloom,
Or dump them in the boggy mire ?
Many oceans came alive again,
My heart now beats between the hopes.
You wanted to make me happy,
And you know that's all I wished for.
Come along with me all the path,
Re-route my steps to your side.
Make those promises and dreams alive,
That I could scream on the mountain,
I got the love I wanted !
I got the life I wanted !

40. Full fledged

Searching for the glitter,
My nights are gearing up.
Footprints of your love,
Still get my eyes on them.
I got your fragrance in my lungs,
Never it will fade, but it must be !
Iam not full fledged, Iam incomplete,
Finding my Destiny, Iam on the way !
Thought you might like my honey,
Made it so sweet. Oh! Oops, you're diabetic !
My love killed your every cell and nerve,
Sorry that medicines too have expiry time !
You were not any sylvian hamster dear,
But I am sure that you are my first love .
You were my oxygen and google maps,
I was your addict, thrown into a dustbin !
Now that I found you don't like my breathe
Knew, all that glitters is not good and gold,
My paths have been shut down,
Endings have been written down,
You know they are incomplete, not full fledged !

41. Together

This evening cool mist,
Is letting me to lose myself,
In your lovely promises.
Shining starry street lights,
Are predicting how glam,
You'll make my life story.
Trees turning backwards,
But wind hitting me meek,
is making this journey sleek.
Rising moon in the sky,
And moving bus tyres,
And I'm thinking that the time,
Would make us soon, together.
Would make us soon, together !

42. New roads

Iam into these new roads,
To explore all the life modes.
I know that Iam now alone,
I do fear and get clumsy.
The lizard on my wall knows it,
Better than your shadows do.
You got the privilege to fly,
Between black and white dens.
See, my wings are cluttered,
And veins clogged with your love.
You hold and leave me in the pace,
And said that our paths dont face.
I know that iam now alone,
I do fear and get clumsy,
Iam into these new roads
To explore all the life modes.

43. This or that

The moon is so beautiful.
Or just a round reflection ?
The nights are so scarifying.
Or just spaces to hide yourself ?
Skies above are limitless.
Or just gas with cotton candies ?
Your eyes have all my world.
Or just arms to lure and illude ?
The shrub roses are giving nectar.
Or just the thorns to bleed the bees ?
I feel so secure in your arms.
Or Just Iam losing my identity ?
We make all squares and rectangles.
Or just circles with molded endings ?
The lines are going significant.
Or just some meaningless phrases ?

44. Bonding thread

I know we are far away,
But It seems there's a thread,
That connects our hearts always.
Fragile but beautiful,
Invisible yet magical,
It pulls me and you together.
You can't see me crying I know,
And I can't see you bearing pain.
Giving us a hope in utter dark,
We both live and would die together.
You understand when I want you to,
And I got used to the way you love.
You are that dew after the summer,
Which adds blood to my dying heart.
We'll hold to this thread always,
And love each other till our hearts get tired.
We'll hold to this thread always !

45. Fireflies

When I see the black night sky,
And rain giving me thunderstorms,
Making my eyes to go hazy,
And I know the path is thorny.
Darker this night is getting,
My moon gets clouds on it,
Shows me light only when it desires.
Stars are losing their small wisdom,
Started to blew off from the sky.
The steps may be slow but steady,
I've got some fireflies to guide me,
Nurture and throw the thorns away.
Finally, I'll make the sun waiting to shine,
Those rains will then be rainbows.
I know moon has no light of its own,
And stars are just much far away.
Fireflies ever lie close by my side.
When the black night comes back again,
And rain will then bloom some smiles,
Because, I've got some fireflies !
I've got some fireflies !

46. Not you totally

It's not your fault that you don't love me.
I desired to grow garden in the desert,
and I can't blame that plants are poisonous.
We were never matching to our hearts,
All that we did was adjusting by force.
You and me don't want to kill each other,
and our eyes to see same dreams together.
Some beautiful days, that we got by mistake,
I want to erase, but they are stubborn to go.
You came and went whenever you wanted,
My heart has a door, you need to remember.
Swinging to your rhythm, I lost in the air.
And I want to loose you now so badly,
That I can loose myself to get you away.
I will not be lingering here all my life,
I don't know if you ever think of my love,
But, I'll be glad if you know that,
I will not be ready to hold your hands again!

47. Under the tree shade

Today under this tree shade,
My memories wont go fade.
Come just sit beside me,
I'll uncover all and you'll see,
what's behind that cloud in the sky,
That makes it to rain and cry.
My story is just like yours and all,
Where you could see springs and fall.
Leaves like people, flowers like friends,
Blossom like lovers, the story never ends.
The wind is hitting gently me and you,
So I believe the facts could do..
Iam so anxious. If you are much eager,
I'll open the pages, hiding is now meagre.
Pick up much empathy from your heart,
it would translate the story, like an art.
I want you to hold my hands as before,
Know the cloud is thirsty above seashore.
Leave me if you want, I can live alone.
And it takes me some time to get on.
Today under this tree shade,
My memories wont go fade.

48. Our heart

It was out to be something beautiful,
Preparing its land to welcome the sky.
Seeds of hopes were in thousands,
Fears and confusions were like floods.
All the continents, oceans and moons,
Looked to fit aptly in these small fists.
But, boundaries too laid down, invisible.
That side of wall looks always beautiful,
Light through the windows is powerful.
It wants to jump and run along the wind,
Like a thread swings though the needle.
It wants to explore all the Highs and lows,
Don't know how much the sugar is sweet,
But, It never wants to skip a love beat.
Its tiny but yet big than the enormous.
Its my heart and yours too !

49. Shapeless pebble

Iam a small, shapeless pebble,
Flowing to your river currents.
I wish to grow up into a mountain,
Make my heart as strong as stone,
All that for making my tears to atone.
I've heard many ickle fishes in you,
Lauding all the love and care you gave.
Did I hurt you or were I, an impurity ?
Or just I was none of your priority ?
You went calm sometimes, and
I got to settle in your deep heart cage.
And I too saw at times, your rushing rage.
People threw me into you always,
And said that I was a part of you.
And took me out of you sometimes,
But, put me back as I appeared futile.
I wish if we could be only us, for now.
Then I would never wish to grow !

50. Closet

I'm getting tired of hiding,
Decorating in my closet.
Spiders nets are so spooky,
That they'll bind all my limbs.
Uh-oh ! The lights are turning off,
And the cabinet space is choking.
Can anyone get me out of this,
Say these closets need some clothings.
There are holes letting some air in,
But my every cell wants to breathe in.
Just like daisies smiling on the ground,
I want to swing and dance around.
That sky is bored having only clouds,
Trees want to bloom some rainbows loud.
Now, I want to build some shelves,
And smash the closets in our lives.
I'm getting tired of hiding,
Decorating in my closet.

51. Beautiful sky

The sky will not seem now, to be pale.
Fishes will fly in the sky high,
Mermaids having stars on the hair,
Will do a heavenly ramp walk.
And your eyes will evince the magic,
Once you choose the right one.
Your smiles, then will be insured.
All your tears will not be left unanswered.
That one will be a little tinker fairy,
Coming from the land of springs,
Will give you its wings and let you free,
From all the thorns that you got stuck in.
Empathetic, but kills all the narcissists.
The sky will now seem to be beautiful,
Even smiles back seeing you happy,
And then, your eyes will evince the magic !

52. Home for us

Thought of building a home,
Where we could stay right in.
Brought concrete, Bricks and sand,
But see, we've made them into walls.
Broken our hearts with love and care,
We can't see any open shut door,
Nor any window to look into our lives.
Can any storm could break this thing ?
Or we want its roots to just stay cling.
The more we let and see it grow,
It would make more, the agony glow.
We would turn into me and you,
Will be unknown, nothing will be due.
Walls will rise above our heights,
We, our, together will perish in nights.
Surrounded by the shadows of wall,
You and me would never hear a scream,
And even make our last goodbye !

53. To my love

Early morning in that bus trip,
My head resting on your shoulder,
Windows closed to stop the wind,
Sharing one blanket, for warmth
I smiled, having all trust in you,
Beautiful as sheep's wool, your hair,
Gave me flying rainbows in the air.

Holding each other's hands always,
I felt happy, being named as your support.
and you then called me Seventy,
Fought for my space, gave me safety.
Knowing you are intolerant to cold,
You always bought ice creams for me.
We had it itty bitty clumsy, sweet and all
But, we never left ourselves for real.

54. Roads of past

The roads we used to walk through,
Now, seem to be got divided.
The old paths have become uncertain,
and our eyes and faces unremembered.
The voyage looks to be at its end,
Even the waves always are fluttering.
We can't fake ourselves all the time,
Our purpose of the union is undefined.
Words sound to be still healing,
But, the wounds appear to be lingering.
Questions disappeared long ago,
Answers appear yet to be digested.
These lines may hint to have a meaning,
Gaining them, you might lose yourself.

55. Chains of love

All the chains of love and friendship,
That we wrapped around ourselves,
are questioning trust and understanding.
Giving us pain and protection,
They give us smiles and also tears.
What for this life, you want to wrap,
or break them all and live alone ?
The greater you want to hold them,
The more you will suffer..
But, love shouldn't hurt, should it ?
The tighter you wrap, it looks toxic.
Love should be like a rose bed,
Thorns may bleed you sometimes,
But, petals should heal you..
Love wants to hold the hands always,
and break the big choking chains !
When every chain blooms into a flower,
All the chains of love and friendship,
That we wrapped around ourselves,
Will define trust and understanding !

56. Disconnected

Searching for the places here and there,
Where I can be myself.
I got tired breathing in your kisses,
Let me love myself more than I love you,
For rest of my life, let me be disconnected.
In this egoistic tragedies of pleasure,
Let me find myself what my heart wants.
There's no people who want me to die,
Until I want them to be in my place.
Understanding has its own price you know,
So, get disconnect and know yourself.
There are talking plants and animals,
Touching winds, waves and birds in the sky.
They'll give us the soothe we're striving for.
So, get disconnect and kill yourself,
Love and live once again, get disconnected !

57. Sweety pie

Hey my dear sweetie pie ,
I fed you like your mother,
guarded you like a father,
I've been close like a brother,
And felt for you like a friend,
And I thought you found safety
In holding my hands together..
I gave you all that i could ,
I could have given my life if you asked,
My love flowers bloomed for you,
But your branches went off from them,
I never wanted to get you haunted,
But I couldn't stop the time and you.
I always wanted to make you happy.
Just because iam not a full moon,
You left me saying i was incomplete.
I wont ask you to come back again,
Neither to hold my creepy hands.
I don't want to kill you again ..
You always had wings to fly high,
But, you stood by me sometimes.
and you have your own life always.
Stay happy my dear sweetie pie !

58. Cherry on the top

I may crave much sweet vanillas,
Chocolate nuts in cool butter scotch,
silky strawberries or any other top notch,
My love always had cherry on its top.
Cause i love it when its red and angry ,
Giving me a chance to make it cosy.
Soothing when it looks into my eyes,
Melts them like it would eat my heart.
Cause i love it when it looks like a child,
My love always had cherry on its top.
I love when it gets crunchy in the first,
But the way it gets sweeter with the time,
So always my love had cherry on its top!

59. Got to move

Days passed and so many nights,
have made me leave all my dreams.
I was a dirty tree to give you flowers,
My branches and roots made me die.
I've been cut back into a twig that day,
But that made me know what is love,
and what soil and rain actually should do
Iam growing into a stubborn red flower,
Got all the fragrances from that dirt ,
Iam getting wings, from all my petals,
to roam around in the sky all alone.
Because all who match me is only me,
I got to move and make all colours shine.
My constellations, to reach are very far ,
I have no time and time does no favour,
I got to move and make all colours shine !

60. Cheap violin

I'm not a cheap violin,
If you didn't wanted to play some lines,
Why did you cut the strings ?
I had love on you so much,
And all you had is hemophobia .
Not every string oozes blood like mine,
Your finger may be teared down then,
And you know it perfectly ,I know !

I gave you all my chords, you know,
But you threw away all the rosin,
Thought I'll give you always melodies,
You even wanted to break the bow.
you had expectations and I had the pain !
I got tuned to your hands always,
You never tried a love theme, did you ?

I thought you were holding me fine,
But all you wanted me to use and throw,
Broken strings but, not just a wood piece,
I'm not a cheap violin,
If you didn't wanted to play some lines,
I say, now, you must go away !

61. End of the sky

I want to reach that end of sky,
before it gets dark in the night.
I want my wings now, back to fly,
and I believe that you'll never lie .
You told me that you'll love me tight,
So be my thread and make me a kite !

Hand in hand it gets so lovely,
A promise for life time really,
Thinking how sweet you'll make it,
I've been building my dreams high.
I found protection in you always,
Grab me too close that you can't leave me,
Pump in love and give me the warmth .

The time is fleeting it's getting late,
You should never make loved ones wait.
The time is fleeting it's getting late,
You should never make loved ones wait.
Come my dear ,come to me close.
Before it gets dark in the night,
I want to reach that end of sky with you ,
I want to reach that end of sky.

62. Purple shade

Have you seen the shade of purple,
Lying somewhere in the rainbows?
Scattered reds and whites are there,
Fighting with each other from times,
to conquer the voices and dawns .
They thought the moon was red & big,
and the white stars were minute and bum.
They never wanted to see above sky,
Setting up limits and borders to fly.
They are decorating haunted closets,
And want everyone to fit into the racks.
Some of the reds got whites some love,
Then, pink allies bloomed like spring.
I wish all our souls could talk together,
and believe purple lies in all our colours

63. It was you

You said that I cry a little while longer,
Than I usually do..
You forgot how my smile looked like,
and how I made you happy.
I like it that you wanted me to vanish,
I'll fulfill your last wish for sure, but
Let me make you hear me one last time..
Make you hear one last time..
You threw me into nights,
Showed me darkness,
Made me lonely, clueless
But you cant stop the east,
Smiling at me with sunshine.
You cant cut me too long,
I know this'll hold no long .
Shadows, and these dark paths,
Will not make me frightened,
Ill find some fairy fireflies,
And they will burn your eyes !
One day you'll scream loudly,
No one could make you happy,
As i shed my tears into water.
You said that I cry a little while longer,
Than I usually do..

You forgot how my smile looked like,
and how I made you happy ,
I like it that you wanted me to vanish,
I'll fulfill your last wish for sure, but
Let me make you hear me one last time..
Make you hear one last time.

64. You don't know dear.

Some silence is making noise,

Every time, deep in my heart.

Nobody else could hear may be,

Anyone never even tried for once.

And I get blew away by some wind,

too weak than my commitment, sometimes

But you dont know dear,

How could you know ?

You never had to be in my place..

Some loving hearts are staying too near,

Tangled too deep, intricated may be.

Farther the thread goes, straighter it is

Easy to cut and to stitch it they say..

But you dont know dear,

How could you know ?

You never wanted to hold the thread,

You never had to be in my place..

Good for one is bad for another may be,

Unless they come in terms with each other.

Day and nights can be best friends even,

Even they dont stay always together.

You will have to give when you expect,

Not losing, not a compromise they say..

But you dont know dear,

How could you know ?
You never wanted us to be complete,
You never had to be in my place...
You don't know dear !

65. Open your heart

Some conversations that
I want to end now, deadly
Some I don't even want to start.
If I put commas in between,
I fear that you'll end the sentence.
Because I know that I am a word,
That you need a dictionary
To understand my spelling.
I'm not complex, neither unknown,
You might misunderstand me.
You just love all the shades of black ,
And foresee the rest hid in the rack.
Iam one made of same twenty six letters ,
Which too made your huge dictionary .
Life will not lie, if you lie within,
Open the pages, open up your heart.
Make my conversations start,
If I put commas in between,
You then complete the sentence .
Try to understand my meaning,
Im just light and easy to pronounce.
Open the pages, open up your heart !

66. The sky I made

So you say that
The sky I made for you
Is ain't beautiful,
You want to stay down,
in the trench for more time,
you seek to be photophobic,
and love that depth even more.
You crave yourself pain,
find pleasure there,
If I desired, I've shown you clouds,
you could be drowned in water ,
I can give you storms and thunder.
Iam a kind of bad hellcat,
I'll make you cry and laugh evil.
I'll not give a chance to cuddle,
and not a second to breathe in,
If I were to show you horror,
it'll succumb you to tragedy.
Now, Iam erasing my limits,
Don't you dare to say that ?
The sky I made for you
Is ain't beautiful ?

67. The blue ocean

Do you know that, this blue ocean
Is bringing tides, wants to touch you,
and make some itty bitty talks ?
Some say it's peace and beautiful,
Others say it's quiet but much dreadful !
You've heard enough everyone's tongues,
But, haven't you heard once your heart ?
Have you made a trial to be together ?
Its then, you know about the ocean,
and the feelings it had for you deep.
The waves seem to hug your footsteps,
It's showing you love and you still fear,
and it's you who thinks they disappear.
The ocean is giving you pearls and corals,
It's you who considered them only stones.
Never went the ocean silent even once,
Day and night, it kept it's currents alive.
Do you understand, the language of love ?
Some say it's hefty and complicated,
But some say it has all the treasures,
You've heard enough everyone's tongues,
But, haven't you heard once your heart ?

68. Rear mirror

When I say you are my moon,
I dont know you are near or far,
The sky is vast and has many stars,
and more than all, a dark background.
That sky and earth may appear close,
But when you look at your back,
The objects in the rear mirror appear
Very closer than actually they are.
You may be very thirsty of love,
Roaming all alone in a vast desert,
If you find anything you want,
I'll tell you that's a mirage or its your dream.
Because objects in the rear mirror appear,
Very closer than actually they are.
Words build words and also the world,
I'll tell you they too, break the hearts.
It's when you get to know what is what,
and objects in the rear mirror appear,
very closer than actually they are !

69. Evil night

In between bats and vampires,
Somewhere in the dark nights,
I would open my eyes to the moon.
Coming out of the goodness box,
I'll show all my evil this bloody night.
Iam very hungry, my blood craves,
Some sweet taste of badness.
You'll tell how cruel actually I am,
When my teeth pierce your meat,
and my venom circulates in you,
picks me up all of your red juice.
Iam eager to hear your screams,
Count the time, the night will end soon.
Feel the smell of mushy ground ,
It's getting wet all with your sweat.
Oh dear, don't fear, I want to gulp you,
So that your dreams will come true.
Remember this world for last time,
when I'll free you from eternal pain,
you can rejoice your new dead life,
Count the time, this night will end soon

70. I know

I know you hate my colours,
and every part of my soul.
Every time I think about love,
It makes me think about you.
Every effort that I've made
to bring smile on your face,
You always made it useless.
Once I turned out as your mirror,
You even hated me much more.
Never understood I held you,
Holding to my bleeding blood
It took me much to write words,
And not as you to utter them.
I always wished to see you smile ,
I've become a villain in your life,
It is pity that my love pains you.
Every time I wanted to forget you,
You get into my damn dreams.
You got other stars in your sky,
Iam not your moon, or any sun,
I know, I don't lie in your memories.
Iam degrading by each day,
My love ain't got any more half life,
Before my soul gets disappear,

It's the time to say goodbye!

71. Love 26 hours

It's not that you are far,
You lie always in my heart
Pushing me from myself,
You filled in me through the time ..
I cannot forget that curly hair
And eyes which protected me
We ran out of time cuddling & fighting
So, we made it twenty six hours daily
Many Ice-creams and Chocolates
Made our memories more sweet
We were both like milk and water
There was nothing as much cuter
This way I thought our story
But you were on your lines, and
Made all my papers burn ..
It makes me to end these lines
Whatever story you make ,
I guess you'll be happy !

72. Be mine

I get close very soon,
that's my strength
When I get connected ,
And I lose myself soon
Around most loved ones.
And that gets me tears ,
When things go upside down..
You can't keep bind your heart
Wings around your loved ones ,
Those limits tear me up ,
I get tired faking expressions ,
And killing all emotions.
When I bear all your words,
It's not that I am weak,
I want you to be in my life ,
Understand, I gave you other chance
to know the things correct .
I want you to be different ,
from all the others, because
I want you to be mine forever .
and make me feel some safe
and let me breath to my heart ,
I want you to be mine forever ,
You are my precious loved one ,

So, I want you to be mine forever !

73. Jar of life

Any fragrance that might be sweet,

Any colour that may be cool ,

Any metal that is shining now ,

Any friendship that is not real ,

have to fade away sometime ..

This day they may look beautiful,

All that they leave is shades of vain ,

Some or other day, they'll give you pain ..

Some stains are removable ,

Some wounds are repairable,

Some words are forgivable. But,

There's no glue to stick the broken heart ,

We can't make the pieces go together..

As if knife has been used for taking butter,

And once the blood oozes out,

It gets more tasty, and the jar gets empty

And once the blood oozes out,

The demon rises in frenzy,

The jar gets totally empty ..

Nothing in this world is permanent,

Neither anything is temporary,

All those lie in our memories forever ,

So in this mean time, try to be happier ,

Just like the jay sings much sweeter..

Everything has to fade away at some time,
Colours, fragrance, butter and the demon,
Leaving the essence of happy memories,
And filling the jar again, one more time..
And filling the jar again, one more time.

74. Everything in you my dear

I'm not rich to get you any suites,
Can't take you round the world in planes,
I'm not white ,either Iam not black
And I don't bother whatever
Skin tone you have anyway ..
I don't want any soft cushions,
I sleep in your lap, softer than the clouds ,
I dont need any tree to swing for me,
Melodies melody than ever in your voice,
There's no wind better than the wind
That lies in your respiration I take..
I dont need apples, apricots and pineapples,
I can't fill my stomach, all with the air,
What I crave is your love, my appetite
Or happy, I can die of hunger in your lap ,
I'm not that daring, I fear in the nights,
It's so hard to step in the dim moonlight,
And stars are making my eyes go fading,
I don't know your hand would let me out,
I don't want you to be strong, and Bright
Together, We will make it out Straight ,
All that we need is hope, trust and Faith ..

We don't need wealth and huge mansions,
For a few feet space and a heart to rest upon,
Am I making this much costly for the life ?
I'm not jealous, but all your love is mine,
So, please come to me, at least for once
Come out from my dreams, for once
I don't need anything anymore ,
I would find everything in you..
Oh oh , I will find everything in you ..

75. Cute cat

Such a cute face ,
With perfectly round eyes ,
I'll be waiting for you to blink ,
To see more beautiful than pink ..
The way you pass swiftly ,
Through the space you swing ,
Fly in the air ,roll and Jump on me ,
Buttery whiskers not like anywhere..
The way that your ears curl ,
Calculate moves and Scratch everyone,
Still get lots of kisses on your paws..
Black, silver, white, fat, fluffy, ginger ,
You steal all our hearts anyway ..
Just a little Meow and you conquer all ,
Such a cute stance,
With perfectly working plot ,
You steal all our hearts away !

76. Golden guns

In this world of golden guns,
I thought I got a shadow
That would protect me
From the dark and Burning lights
I forgot that nights are there
You would disappear, leave me all alone
Hopeless, I remain counting each second
And the stars far away in the sky
Until you return, because I believe
you bring me some Sunshine ..
When I look into your eyes
Every time I saw two bright moons
I felt proud than this earth a lot..
When you said I'll be always with you
You drove all my anxieties away,
We went all along the roads together
Always inseparable from each other
And by the time you made me your maniac
And I became your never ending phobia ,
It's the time we need to wrap the things
And me to take my heart out from your curls
You would disappear finally from my world
My dear one of the golden guns ..
My dear one of the golden guns..

77. Book

You always said that
All your space was mine,
Which I could always fulfill...
You handled them all ,
My smiles and my tears ..
You were never totally blank ,
You were what I ever wrote..
You came with me along ,
All the lines I made on you,
You never asked me why..
Teared you into pieces ,
threw you down sometimes ,
But you always made to my heart,
Like no one else could do ..
You taught me lessons ,
You suffered pain for me ,
And all I gave you is Ink scars ..
We have our souls connected, and
You never stopped my pen..
For being my sweet silent nook,
Thank you my dear Book !

78. It could have been good

It could have been good
If words were only words,
And we had power to forget
Everything and everyone
Emotions couldn't enter
And crumble our hearts
It could have been good
If you were only you
we don't knew each other
And our eyes don't memorize ..
But, We still see stars in daylight
Blindly ,Starting a page of love
Step into selfish world of dreams..
Hoping for a blue ocean glint
And get stuck in the boggy mire ..
It could have been good
If we understand that
It's not love that gets defeated ,
Love will never disappear in the air
It's the fragrance that gets fade away
It's not that Hearts never change,
Drivers make accidents not the vans
It could have been good
If we understood each other

Before the last leaf got dried
It could have been good
If we said it's never late today
If words were only words,
And we had power to forget
Everything and everyone

79. Complete lines

It melts right here
Deep in my heart
Just when you say hello,
I feel relieved when
I see love emoji's that
You've text me back..
It feels that I can't say
You and me anymore,
We both make a single soul,
Sweeter than any sugar bowl.
Oh darling repeat after me,
Hold my hand dear ,
Cut me into parts
And savour my love
You will never be hunger ever ..
All I want you to give me
Some love that would
turn into ink and I'll
Make my love lines complete ..
Never I walked along
In the nights with you ,
Never I had your hands
Wrapping my body
So close in your hugs ..

But, I always been thinking
How amazing it is ,
All I want you to give me
Some love that would
Turn into ink and I'll
Make my love lines complete ,
Just make my life lines complete !

80. I knew it

I know that you didn't loved me,
And were finding ways to make me out
From the heart ,that I found for this life.
But these nights don't know it ,
And stars are twinkling there still
Stopping sun from making next day .
I know that I didn't make a memory ,
That you ever wanted to keep alive.
But these Robins don't know it
And they get me remind about you ,
Singing our story on the branches
In my garden, On the lonely tree .
I know that I ain't beautiful, curvy
That your hands wanted to grab in ,
And I ain't your gorgeous dream boy ,
But my heart doesn't know it
And keeps on asking for your love
It's losing its beat , on its end to die.
On its end to die, losing its rhythm,
I got tired asking you to listen,
You made me a call on hold, which
You would never lift to answer .
I don't know that you need some pain,
So, you've got to love that guy,

Who would dump you in the path,
And then you come to me and yell ,
Cry and weep on my dead heart,
And say I don't know that you loved me
This deep that I would love you back,
I don't know that you loved me
This deep that I would love you back..
But, I know that you didn't loved me !

81. Love story

Days and nights always
Will come and go ..
Not just black and white,
Not in the sky ,
And not on the earth,
Just look into my eyes
And you'll find the space
That you always wanted
And dreamt deep and high
Come just forget everything
Friend and foe ,
And everyone who used the knife,
I'll show you what love is ,
Just give me a seed dear
And I'll bloom the garden for you.
Where you can sleep calm
And I'll sing you lullabies .
I've got butterflies and bees
to take us into the skies above
And let us put the world down ,
Come just grab my hand dear,
Let us give some shine to sun,
Just look into my eyes and
I'll make for us a sweet home

Honey ,I just want some happiness,
That is hidden in your smiles
I just want you to make me happy
So, give it me for the lifetime.
Together is always beautiful ,
Let we make a great story
That lovers in the past would
rather die of jealousy ...
Dear, just look into my eyes
And let's start the love story .

82. Moon in the sky

When I look at the moon ,
Going on change every night,
And sky never wears blue all the time,
Pink and yellow, red to purple,
Black and rainbow coz it ain't static
Since all yesterdays will not be today
But sky be the sky and so the moon..
Today you see a dreaming seed ..
Fruit or flower, dead or dried
Tomorrows cant be decided dear.
Colours and Shades never mean the heart,
What lies within always makes the art..
Between the boundaries there lies the space,
Beyond the closed window, you then see the world ..
Extremes are not always validated ,
But, Sense in the lines never will go blind,
Because learning is for things and
Love is for knowing souls..
But, sky be the sky and so the moon ..
And, sky be the sky and so the moon ..

83. On your side

Sitting on the side of you,
I smell the love in your breath
And my head found a spot
On your shoulder to bend and rest,
My hand that hugs in your hand
Is Pumping love to my heart
And making it to stay alive ..
Baby, I swear that this is
Going darker than nights..
Making my forehead wet ,
With your kisses, my eyes
Harvest them as tears that
Bind these moments in them..
And my hairs which swing to
Wind just paused to the touch
Of your hand and slept for a while..
This love is turning into lullaby
Baby, I swear that this is
Going sweeter than the dreams..
The steps of my soul which
Are making it together with your path
Are finding new ways to live and
It feels like it should never end
Lillies and roses never bloom

In night , who said that ?
The story should stay sustain
Healing all the past and killing pain ,
Baby, I swear that this is
Going long than seven seas
Come ,let's sing until heaven sees
Baby, I swear ..

84. Empty emotions

My emotions are going empty ..
The scar that you've made on this heart,
Is breaking the world into two,
One far away from the other..
You with the rest lie on the one ,
I would live alone in other..
Clouds of inexistent disparities
Are drilling the space much deeper..
And love losing the sun underneath,
Is screaming at hope for the help..
Flowers are drying up to the shade,
Of the trees on which they first saw the sky ..
Iam escaping from your sights and Calls ,
Missing those peaceful sleeps in your lap..
Shadows of your hatred are growing,
And I remained seeking it's shade always ..
But, You were to fill my soul upto its brim,
With never ending love and happiness,
That never even happened in my dreams.
I can't explain what my feelings are now,
I can't make you stand for this all alone,
My emotions are going empty..
Driving me from your world forever,
Not seeking for any other shadow again,

For finding happiness within,
My emotions are going empty

85. Tinkerbell

Nights get better
When you have the moon with you,
Not in the sky ,it
Lies in my heart and it's you..
Evenings and sunshine
Look a lot more Prettier,
No need of rainbows
I find all the colours in you ..
Love has a fragrance,
Your words are it's elements,
It Makes me smell happy
That I see roses in my heart
Are blooming now High…
Sticking all the shattered
Broken pieces like a glue ,
You make a wonderful
Ally, my Tinkerbell…
You make a wonderful
Ally, my Tinkerbell..

86. Strangers

My heart is waning up and down,
Days are ending up like in a blink.
Dried rivers are getting filled up,
Lights in my dreams are drowning down.
New birds are nesting on the tree,
My memories aren't letting you free.
Stars in the sky are setting night
Burning sun rays are still in my sight.
Orchids are piling up in meadows ,
I remain nowhere around your shadows.
It's been long we aren't together,
Becoming known strangers forever !

87. Little bird wants to sing

A little bird wants to sing,
Opening wings out to swing.
Glazing up to the skies blue up,
Out of the closet, efforts piled up.
To acknowledge the aspirations,
Let thou know the hidden rainbows.
The pinions are dwindling to gales,
And heart is Rushing ahead of hiccups.
Deeper oceans came then together ,
to hear what clams could trill whether .
A little bird wanting to sing,
Then opened a world of beautiful zing !

88. Dear butterfly

Oh dear butterfly,
Why do you fly so high?
My emotions are Subtle,
So are your wings .
Let the sky take some space,
And clear the hazy pace.
Until your rushing juice calms,
Come and rest in my palms.
As always the time is fleating,
To make a mellow, the heart is waiting.
Oh dear butterfly,
Why do you fly so high ?
Lay and Rest sometime,
Close your wings and sleep to the chime !

89. Life of a seed

The seed saw its first sky then,
Days turned today so fast that
Now, the birds chirp on the tree.
Gusts have been defeated,
Shrills now are becoming a lullaby
And The tree busses them with glee.
After, the woods went fracturing..
The bole started trembling then,
To the breathe of the lightest wind !
Time came to fall over and rest,
The tree then turned into timber
Fruits, flowers, and shade remembered.
Driven wherever wind took it,
The seed again saw its first sky.
To embed its roots of eternal joy,
In this temporary lives of hope, ahoy !

90. Love could give sweet

Back in the night,
Seeking moonlight,
My heart beats much fast
Pushing me into pain..
Asking every moment
This is what ultimate
Love could give sweet..
Burning red oceans,
and Shining blue roses,
Melting hot snow flakes
And sun hating shadows..
This is what ultimate
Love could give sweet..
Missing the current
And crying for pain,
Left in this void oh
Seeking for moonlight ,
Back in the night
My heart beats much fast
Pushing me into pain..
This is what ultimate
Love could give sweet!

91. You and me

Butterfly and the flower,
Sky and the cloud,
Moon and the stars,
Rain and the Rainbow,
Pencil and the Paper,
Salt and the Pepper,
Needle and the thread,
Sweet and the sour,
Spring and the Summer,
Lock and the key,
Are the inspiration for
You and Me .

92. We

We know each other,
We don't meet .
We understand each other,
We don't talk.
We care each other,
We don't Bother
We love each other,
We don't live together.
We love each other,
We don't die together.

93. Places

Those are beaches,
Where my heart becomes an ocean.
Those are holiday spots ,
Where my tears get forgotten
Those are pilgrimages,
Where my every smile becomes a rose.
Those are Hot spots,
Embedding all my diverse emotions !
Those are Rome in everyplace ,
Jesus lies here, where my bestie lives !

94. Dear you

Dear you ,
You killed my dreams,
You killed my hopes,
You killed my emotions,
You killed my expressions,
You killed my tomorrows,
You killed my soul ,
But I wonder ,
How do you make dead to talk ?

95. Flower and the bee

He went away from the heart,
The fly now hates the flower,
Which once bloomed for him.
Breaking all the petals,
He has opened his wings .
The flower is dry to sing,
The bee got back his sting .
The fly now hates the flower,
Which once bloomed for him.
This life is too short to remember,
The bee has nothing more to linger .
The life is too short to be longer,
The bee has nothing more to linger .
He went away from the heart,
The flower now hates the flower,
Which once bloomed for him !

96. Our mother

She didn't gave us birth only once.
Whenever we got injured,
she was the one who killed the pain.
Whenever we felt alone,
she was the one who cried for us.
She may doesn't understand us sometimes,
but she is the one who lives for us.
She is the one who never made us to feel low.
Yes! She is the one who is most ignored by us.
She is our mother!

97. Darling, you're mine !

Darling ,
Your hugs are only mine .
Your anger is only mine .
Your kisses are only mine .
Your curly hair is only mine .
Your sweat smell is only mine .
You are only that Thing ,
Which I could say is " Mine ".
You are my only teddy .
You are only my teddy.
If my eyes catch you with someone ,
I can't tolerate ,
Without killing that person on spot ,
I can't tolerate !

98. My dear heart

Hey my dear heart ,
Why don't you speak out ?
Just like other people ,
Why don't you say it bold ?
are you that coward ,
To say " Leave me alone"?
Are you that hardworking ,
To bear my tears alone ?
Oh heart , I beg you..
Make me Heartless !

99. Being a girl

Being named as soft ,
But said to be tough
Being a girl is not Easy .
Being named as Mother
But are often aborted ,
Being a girl is not Easy .
Being named as Beautiful ,
But burning in acids
Being a girl is not Easy .
Being named as Adhishakti ,
But are most molested
Being a girl is not Easy .
Being a girl is Blessed thing !

100. Good friends

Good friends are like smiles,
Who vanish Tears.
Good friends are Those,
Who you remember first,
When you are sad .
Good friends are Those,
Who Stand by you,
In your goods & odds.
Good friends are Those,
Who always stay in Your Heart.
Good friends are Those,
Who are Given by God!

101. Who are you?

Who are you ?
A cute child to my eyes..
Criminal in my thoughts..
Who had stole my soul.
Clown in my sadness,
Dawn to my dark nights.
Season to bloom my love,
The only Reason to live.
We ate vanillas,
We loved strawberries.
Hand in hand,
We saw fairylands.
Such were yesterdays,
I was a part of you ,
You were a part of me.
Today, you are apart from me..
Who are you ?
My dear .. who are you ?

102. Thank you !

To the stars and the sky above,
Which saw my tears when he left me all alone,
To all my friends and now foes,
Who heard my screams when he went deaf!
To all the places where We've been,
Which reminds me of his and my stories,
To my dear lover once upon a time ,
Who made me realize what life is,
To all the near and dear ones,
Who always stood by my side,
To my dear soul which got tired,
But never complained anytime,
To my loving and caring parents,
Who once told It was good If I died,
To all the fake people in my life
Who made me stand and cry all alone,
Thank you !

103. Let them leave

You may want to stay together always,
You both talk, laugh and enjoy all the time,
You will be their first if they are in any need.
Well, you can be treated like a customer care.
But you'll see them walking far away, and
Sometimes, you'll only have the sky to see you cry.
You want them to know all your emotions even tiny,
And they're good at keeping things secret from you,
They've got multitasking in making friends,
They'll close your tab swiftly and open another new.
But you should learn that they've got something,
And You are just little more than nothing.
They've got much better persons on the line,
And they can even say you to step out sometimes,
You give them all your time and love,
And they don't even give a fuck when you're low,
You're desperate for them, you're mad,
They're busy in finding ways to avoid you.
When you get tired waiting for them,
And they'll make you to go all the way alone,
When you feel that you're being used and dumped,
When you don't get the same as much as you give
You should know they are good at acting,
And their film just got an oscar for cheating

You should just sit quite and watch them leave,
You should let them leave !

• 127 •

104. We all have to know

We have to know that we'll be strangers one day,
All the memories that we had good and bad,
Will not help us to utter a word when we meet again.
We have to shake our hands like robots do,
And fake a dozen smiles for the sake of formality.
We know that we would never be able to go back again,
To the times and places where our smiles were real.
We have to find new friends being incognito,
And old friend's shoulder seems thousand miles away.
We know what is truth and what makes a drama,
Yet we are clinging hard to live in our fake dreams.
We know that the world around is watching us,
But our eyes still can't make it to our hearts.
We feel like we know everything within and beyond,
There are million diverging speculations for a single dot,
We know that all the birds don't fly equal in the sky. But,
Everyone wants life to be on their views & perceptions.
All the knowledge we have is to be stored and improved,
And we all have to know that we'll be strangers one day !

105. Juliet don't worry

The same story goes between the lines,
No matter how many ways I write.
I know he ain't built for my type,
And I'm not worth at all for any hype.
I know he can't love me as I wish,
And he's not gonna search for me if I miss.
He's got curly hair and many blondes in his heart,
He'd bleed my heart and I still call it an art !
I know everything about him I think,
And he proves me wrong everytime I blink.
He's got a bunch of roses ready in his pocket,
Ready to throw them on every chic like a rocket.
He cared me like a child when we first met,
He does this still, but I still find ways to be upset.
He's sweet, chubby, much cute and awesome,
Pretty much everything any girl could ask for.
Hope I'll get someone for me,
Who would love me as me,
And there won't be any hurdles in the story,
Romeo please say " Juliet don't worry ! "

106. Hard for me

You gave me all that you've could,

And sometimes pushed me down the hill.

I would run around you like a psycho,

And you'd yell at me when I smiled.

I saw you having another story,

And some other person making my day.

I'm not that what I mean to you,

And you still do want to stick with me.

I think you get now, what's in my mind,

But it turns out that I'm wrong again.

When I call you late in the midnight,

Text you words all from my heart,

And you don't even dare to reply,

It's hard for me to just sit around you

Watching you hanging around with someone new.

There's also a thing that makes me alive,

And that's the heart which is same as you.

It's hard to forget all the things we did,

It's hard to just say that it was a phase.

It's hard to just see in your eyes and not to cry.

It's hard to believe that we'll have to go away,

And then comes a time, we'll be strangers one day.

Can I find someone again lovely more than you?

But, It's hard for me to stop finding you in them !

107. Tell me why?

I know that our days were over,
I saw sun leaving the sky yesterday,
I cried and slept last night,
Woke up and it became today.
That tree lost some leaves a day before,
And it's getting new buds on it again.
I have many other dreams to get them real,
But, I still can't forget you how hard I try.
Tell me why ?
You told you loved someone earlier,
And I saw you making up with some other.
You didn't told me anything either,
And you left me when I wanted you to be my lover.
You never saw me cry,
You never cared what's in my heart.
When I sorted things and moved out,
You come back and asked me to smile.
Tell me why ?
Iam tired of faking all the emotions,
Staring at unanswered questions,
And putting you in trouble with my problems.
You were the first person to hit my heart,
It's broken but you still stay like an art.
Don't you know that we can't be just friends,

When I ask you what's between us,
You always try to skip, but still catch my hand
Tell me why ?
You can go away and have a good life,
I'll sit all the night and decide,
I'll stay very far from your eye sight,
I'll never peek into your personals again,
But, Still get you in my eyes all the day,
No matter how hard I yell and cry,
Tell me why ?

108. My sort of you

It seemed like you left me,
And I fell apart.
No one to see me crying,
Coz you were the only one.
I got some friends who stood by me,
And I called you bad sometimes.
I thought It was over between us,
And went becoming a stone.
Then sometimes you came and went,
Let me hold your hand again,
And lean my head on your shoulders.
I know that's your tolerance,
But that's again my foolishness.
You seem to be getting close to real me,
I told you every inch of my storyline,
Yet you never know what runs in me.
You are just like a small baby,
Cute and innocent, mischievous.
Everytime I want to put an end,
You make it a comma and continue,
You're really good and I can't just act.
It seemed like you left me,
And I should know that.

109. Through the window

I see them through the window,
Playing with someone again.
I know I'm so stupid sitting in the room,
Still want to cry and blame them.
I know we aren't made for each other.
They say we're friends, I know we're not.
I think we're more than just they say,
And at the end, they'll make me a stranger.
Everytime I think that it'll get better,
We'll never leave a chance to mess it up.
I get gifts from them on my birthdays,
And scars that take long time to heal.
They say they deserve their freedom,
But they're ready to erase my borders.
I do get certain abrupt unasked apologies,
Like to fix a cracked wall with a tape.
I see them through the window,
But, not in my heart when I close my eyes.
I see them through the window,
Slowly moving on and going awry.

110. koala, teddy & blackberries

Fond of blackberries,
I ate from someone's backyard.
Sometimes sweet and sometimes sour.
When fence broke my legs,
I went far and saw a cute white teddy bear.
It came and gave a hug and said,
You can make a garden, I'll lend a hand.
Don't worry we'll stay together it said,
Took me to a forest, far from everyone,
Left me all alone and asked if I was fine.
Teddy said berries were always sweet,
But I was numb to enjoy their pleasure.
Gifting me a warm rug,
Saying goodbye,
Teddy said it wanted some freedom.
There was a koala bear I occasionally pet,
With heart like a golden retriever.
But like berries, I know it ain't mine.
Sweet or sour, berries filled my stomach.
Good or bad, teddy sometimes made my day.
Sitting at the top branch,
Koala saw all this and smiled at my face !

111. You are like everyone

You came to me when I was left alone,
You heard my silly stories and said it'll be fine.
I thought I've got someone pure as gold,
And I assumed you'd never leave me in the cold.
You praised me for being a good friend,
Said everyone was bad guy and then held my hand.
You were much near, sweet as a strawberry.
Said everyone used me, I sorted my priorities.
I remained same all the time from when we met,
But,you hated the person for the reason you loved,
Like Tay's "Indie record that's much cooler than mine".
You then sticked on to another friend,
When I asked, you said that you seek freedom.
Gave me gifts, but forgot me as a person.
I hope that your circle of choosing ends,
And you may find a stable nest to rest in.
You read my silly poems and said it'll be fine.
Now you left me alone like every one did !

112. The same story

It's been a year since we met last time,
And your eyes still got that same shine.
I've been on a word that we are over, but
You melted me like ice when you came over.
New ones in my life remain as new ones, and
Old friends go and come into my heart sometimes.
You said that I should be on my own, see
I got deceived by somebody who see me as a clown.
My heart gets broken again,
And I tend to keep it on a repeat mode .
It's hard to keep the doors always shut,
And atlast, I forget the keys to enter my house.
I always think to improve my story line,
But each and every time, I had to kill some characters.
It's been a year since we met last time,
And my freaking story remains the same !

113. Don't try again

You used to curl your fingers into mine.
Pluck my cheeks and tell that I'm cute.
You used to rest your head on me,
Sleep on my side and ask if it's okay.
I didn't asked you to do them all.
But, when I do the same in return,
You say that I'm mentally deprived.
And label me as chaotic.
You shout as you want on me,
hug and ask me to feed you.
You tell others that I'm your bestie,
And tell my mother that I'm not raised properly.
You know my favorite enemies,
And tell them that I cook good food.
You know that I love you, and
You gifted me a shirt with your ex.
Yes, I know I'm incomplete.
Yes, It won't be full-fledged.
Yes, I'm Bitching a lot about you
And you'll find me cursing you
With my friend in our chats.
Things are good if you do,
And whatever I do will be bad.
You used to curl your fingers into mine,

Now don't try, I'll break even your ribs &, spine!

114. maisie, taylor and meghan

Going on roads somewhere,
Spending all the time like shit,
Having nothing left in my head,
I act like drunkard, psycho maniac.
Seeing the sky in the nights,
Closing my eyes to look more black.
Trying to act good all say,
And I know, I got no shame till today.
Endless playlists of feminism,
Are always a flamboyance,
Maisie, Meghan, taylor always slay.
I know some bragging greedy goats,
I bet they're even blind at toilet etiquette.
Writing silly lines everytime,
Going on roads somewhere,
I'm treating all the time like shit

115. Someone new

I'm going places with someone new,
I'm making my calls to you go few.
But, why all tell me that I get your name,
Every day, now and then, I got no shame.
You come in my dreams, who asked you to do ?
I'm getting close to others, you never asked who.
You hang up with me all the days and say it's good.
You leave me in the dark and ask why not I should ?
You hardly see me as some close friend sees,
You know my secrets and act like I speak Japanese.
I brag that I knew everything about you,
And you even don't care to know my full name.
I'm not your first thing and likely so goes for you.
But, we are the best thing happened to each other,
I can say, because we can't resist this distance.
Closing my haunted heart for a renovation,
And setting emotional spider webs on fire,
I'm going places with someone new !

116. Tinkerbell & Ally

On that night, over a phone call,

She got to know my love story.

She took a sec, she came back again.

She wasn't close to my heart before,

But the way she kept me close,

And didn't poop over my mind anytime,

Said that we all are same at the end,

She then climbed into my heart.

Knew nothing then, but never judged,

She tried to be a learner and an ally.

She said our hearts both cling lub dub,

When she got dumped by her love partner,

And now, we're writing poems together,

Laughing and Cursing our love mates.

On that night, over a phone call,

If she didn't knew my love story,

And she didn't came back again,

I would not be here to write these lines !

117. I know

Too long that I've been trying,

Trying hard to ace like you in leaving.

But tell me why Iam still cursing,

And finding you always in my routine ?

Tell me what you want to make me into,

As I get to hear you like my old ringtone.

This heart is growing numb on your name,

And finding other companies go same.

Now I know,there's no bandages for my maim.

Then I suddenly realize I was given no pain.

Worst days and best togethers all will go in vain,

Now I'm 23 and I grew more dumb than 21.

I know love and I know hate .

I know good and I know bad.

I know you and I know me.

I'm a meat piece, fat sprinkled over.

See what I'm turning into and

Tell me what you want to make me into !

118. False hopes

You let me touch your curly hair,
And I thought that love is in the air.
You said we make weekends go good.
And we had five worst days in a row.
You took me wherever you used to go,
But when I need, you never made a move.
You tell me that you'll be always with me,
But I see you always wanted me to flee.
You were that sugar coated sweet candy,
I was that dumb boy who cried daily.
Tell me, Was it you or was it me ,
Who started giving me those false hopes .
Lately, but we set ourselves now free,
Tell me, Was it you or was it me
Who started giving me those false hopes .

119. Stranger, kiss my heart!

Hey stranger, come kiss my heart.
We've got snakes hissing on our back.
Don't close your eyes until,
You get to trust my hands.
I've been through all the way,
And you must be from the hills.
We'll get to know each other,
We'll get to see the sun shine.
Hey stranger, come look in my eyes.
We've got something to share.
Don't utter a single word,
When you see a wagging tail.
Shadows can't tell shapes and sizes,
But we know diamonds and spades.
We'll roam around together,
We'll get along together.
Someday, we'll become strangers.

120. No difference

Lazy mornings, sweet and scary dreams.
You seem to stop coming into them.
Many new faces I've seen after you,
Some nice and chubby like persimmons.
I wanted to lay roads of love to some hearts,
And desire cuddling all the days and nights.
You raised my love threshold so high,
That when they start wrapping me with their hands,
My heart just switches to aeroplane mode.
I've been blamed of acting like a good boy,
Like you did and I get to realize that you all do,
Now I want to take the advantage.
Lazy mornings and alone journeys,
You seem to add no difference to them !

121. Bad blood

Been told that some guys are bad,
If I won't woke up this day,
They'll use me as they want,
And I'll give them my amazon prime free.
Thanks for telling fella,
You saved my day.
But, I see you giggling,
On seeing my face, with that bad guy,
Making more meanings with them.
I've been looking to hear me,
On everyone's tongues,
But, everyone make me the bad guy,
And at the end, I remain blamed.
It's been pleasure and I enjoy,
To be called as a bad guy.
Been told that some guys are bad,
You'll just turn bad and Iam,
Ofcourse, we all have "bad blood" !

122. From a doctor

To all the suffering and crying crowd,
My apron somehow gave them the hope.
Amidst their loud whines and groans,
My stethoscope could also hear their heart beats.
Placing my hands on their wrists and taking pulse,
I also made them to trust me every second.
I had patience to hear their every misery,
And courage to treat, from my big fat books.
Countless days of irregular appetites,
Night outs and travelling to every library rack,
Counting bones and days I had enough sleep.
All the suffering I have gone through,
Vanish when they call me "Doctor".
Black and white, rich and poor,
Men and women, straight and LGBTQIA,
My eyes only see their hope when they come to me.
To all the suffering and crying crowd,
Who only see me as a healing machine,
I too have my own life and families,
Iam a human and I also deserve dignity.
Piling all the scars that patients make,
Being a doctor is not a piece of cake.
To all the suffering and crying crowd
Iam a ray of hope, I'm the doctor of cope.

123. Strangers

We were strangers at first,
Hesitating to talk.
Slowly like the rising seed,
We made our paths so close.
Holding our hands,
We stood always side by side.
You and I and I and You
We were both together,
And we didn't needed anyone.
I was dumb and made our story.
Realised that I ain't even your friend.
You used me like everyone did,
And I got no shame.
When I demanded love from you,
And I know now It's a mirage.
I just got to know it clear,
When I look onto the sky,
We're just like moon and the venus.
Close on the outer side,
Embedding much farness,
That's out of our expectations.
Slowly like the wilting plant,
We made our paths closed.
Hesitating to talk,

We became strangers as first.

124. I got tired

Hey.. I got tired.
Writing poems in the late nights,
Refraining to ask someone's hand.
I thought it's easy as you do,
To Forget your name and all your things.
But, when I'm in the middle of a crowd,
Talking to someone I want to call "Oh Dear !"
Then my lips betray and utter your name.
I saw you for the first time and we spoke. But,
I don't really remember how you got into my heart.
Hey.. I got tired.
I know it's tough for us to be stick together.
Our tastes don't match ,
But we ate always together.
We're both norths of a magnet,
But we stood always together.
You were summer and I was winter,
But our love went extreme together !
Hey.. I got tired.
Calling you everytime I felt low,
Knowing that you never care.
Cursing you for leaving me all alone,
Knowing that I don't have the dare
Still writing my silly, senseless lines,

Knowing that you don't even read,
Still waiting for your reply, No!
Hey.. I got tired,
I got tired !

125. Story ended

I know our story has ended.
But, everytime something goes wrong with me,
I remember your name and want to blame you.
Still think if you were here, would make things good.
And would wrap me in your hands like in the past.
Like our bond was sweet first and then got rot,
Faces are changing and their flavours are sour.
Journeys will be smoother and sweeter,
If you have the right one sharing the path.
Thorns will not make your blood to bleed,
If their finger makes your pain to close.
I don't know who should be on my side,
And I ask why should they ever be.
I fear if I'd have another you in them,
And sometimes have me in them !

126. Loved you because

Loved you because you cared me a lot,
You protected me like a baby,
You held my hands when I was falling down,
You made me feel so special my dear !
When I showed my scars,
You turned them into wounds.
You said I was cute but you left me when I smiled.
You play with my heart,
But you don't like when I touch your hair !
What should I do, I find you always in the air.
Should I stop my breathe or bound my space ?
Darling you live your life as you wanted.
Don't try to peep into my haunted heart,
You'll see a dead red rose plant.
It's thorns will pluck you and you'll bleed.
And you know I can't see you sit and cry.
Loved you because It stuck up in my heart,
That your heart had a place for me somewhere.
No problem honey, we already had goodbye !

127. Just

Walls are just walls now.
Places we've been to are in my heart,
I don't remember the hand I wanted to hold.
Long lasting conversations and rare gifts,
Alone nights and everything forgotten.
All my first times with you are just first times,
Beaches attract me more than our bond.
Your house and mine are always far,
As you said, our routes are separate.
People are just living shadows,
My heart wants to grow thorns.
Your voice is just a street dog howl,
And mine was always a snake hiss.
Your eyes are just two meat balls,
And my fat flies high in the sky.
Walls are just walls now,
We are just you and me now !

128. Teach me

I'm done fighting with you,
I can't even fight with myself now.
Can you teach me how to forget,
About you and everything you've done ?
Every time I want to go away,
You stretch your hands to me.
When I want to take a nap there,
You prick my heart and then killed me !
I know it's all over between us,
I can't even say something started.
We are just two red hearts of hatred,
But something stopping us to say "No".
I know we aren't lovers ,
We are not even fit to be friends !
I know we hurt each other a lot ,
But it's hard to say goodbye.
Can you teach me how to forget?
Coz I'm done fighting with you,
I can't do all this for my life time,
Hug me or come, stab my heart !

129. I gave.

Gave someone my time, someone my money.
Gave everything they asked for all the time.
I've been called their support and good friend sometimes.
They call me bad guy If I leave them once,
But can't remember how many times I was deserted.
I've been a dice in their hands in the yesterdays,
They say they're good because they let me live !
I cried in corners all the nights seeing the stars above,
Always hoped that someone would wipe my tears.
I feel that I always play the victim card,
And make them villains in my stories.
I know that I'm a bitch shaking my ass allover,
Now being called bad gives me much pleasure,
Like my wings liberated will cut all their tongues !
Gave someone my heart, someone my life.
Gave up everything I desired and all my dreams,
Now I'll give what I want and take zero fucks !

130. On the beds of memories

On the beds of memories,

Let you and me take some rest.

We know that we aren't made for each other,

You are east and I'm not your summer.

We want us to smile, but not together.

Not holding hands now, not much to bother.

Your eyes still have the same shine,

And our hearts have the same hatred.

We will be going far in opposites,

Having hands still stretched to our hometown.

Wanting to be madly caring each other,

We never even seen us weeping in the corner.

You have your secrets and I have mine.

Not much we talk, when walking on the roads.

There's nothing between us or we love silence.

The best gift that we gave ourselves,

That we have blood oozing from our hearts.

Laying some bandages over the wounds,

On the beds of memories,

Let you and me take some rest !

131. Phone

You know everything,
You clear my every doubt.
You sing songs for me,
You show me the correct way,
When I get lost.
You are always with me,
And you know the things I like.
You never judge me like others do.
You are my light in darkness,
Only connection I have,
When I want to stay all alone.
We spend all the day together,
And you sleep next to me in the night.
You cheer me up,
And I'll charge you up in return.
Happy friendship day my Phone !

132. You belong with me.

And say " You belong with me " .

• 161 •

133. The sky was blue

The sky was blue,

Clouds are passing,

Birds, singing as usual.

You came then,

In your favorite outfit,

On a friday.

Made your hand go curved on my shoulder,

Said I look good when I smile,

You said that you never lied.

Butterflies and many flowers,

Saw us always together.

And everything was good,

The sky was blue,

Clouds are passing,

Birds, singing as as usual.

But, then I got a thing in my heart,

Hitting me hundred times,

What if it takes you more to love me than to hate me?

Would you like my heart as it is,

Or with a ton of make-up ?

I'm not used to this,

You and all your things,

I Can't fit them up in my wardrobe.

You said our ways are not in the same way,

And my smile has a foul smell.
I understand and go away,
You again then want to hug me,
What if it takes me more to love you than to hate you?
You and me,
Have no glue,
To hold us together !
The sky is blue,
Clouds are passing,
Birds, singing as usual.

134. Wish I was

Wish I was just a blue spot in the sky,
Or one of the leaves that look always green.
Being in a rainbow bleeds their eyes,
And my chlorophyll can take all colours.
Wish I was just a smoke from an old city car,
Or one of the ants which go in a line.
City people don't get to see fresh air,
And not any rain bugs visit us in summer.
Wish I was just a water drop in an ocean,
Or one of the moths and butterflies.
Fishes even reside in darkest depths,
And bats come out of caves rarely.
Wish I was just true to myself,
And live like other haters do !

135. A place for everyone

The sky above smiles at me,
I wonder what's above the clouds.
It says" You can only touch me,
When the wings are your's and
It's hopeless when you look for other's. "
The sun in the sky shines bright,
Turns here and looks in my eyes,
Tells " You can make everyone happy,
But only you can make you happy,
Not even your shadow could do it,
In a way better than you do !"
Flowers in my garden bloomed today,
Dancing to the eastern winds,
Sing " We grew up from our closets,
It's too hard to hide from the world.
We are valued because we shine,
And bloom like a butterfly,
Crushed, if we were a caterpillar ".
The world is so bad to live everyone say ,
But, the world is made by the same voices,
Praised and oppressed,
Celebrated and cursed,
Humiliated and hugged,
Everyone and everything has a place here to stay!

136. Hit song

You were to be a hit song in my playlist,
That I could hear all the time in a week,
And say I knew your lyrics after some time.
Then replaced by another new song in a row.
But, you became my permanent caller tune,
And the song my ukulele strings would cling to.
I would have you all the time in my spotify playlist,
You would be an old piece for my headphones,
But, my ears always want to hear your rhythm.
I want to sing you on my uke soul forever,
We'll try different chords and strumming patterns.
And it'll sound melodious out of our hearts
You are a hit song in my playlist,
That I could hear all the time in my life.

137. We – but not today

We talk for hours on the phone,
We share stories over instagram.
We laugh about some shitty joke,
We talk about building our houses,
And living side by side in a big city.
You call me at seven in the morning,
You wish me in midnight on my birthday.
And I think that you really care. But,
When I really wanted you to be with me,
I never even found your shadow near me.
I'm grateful that you shared my smiles,
and I know that I'm not your responsibility.
Everybody and I know that you are good.
But, please don't name me as your close friend.
Now, that you and me know each other well,
I'll be never asking you to hold my hands again.
And will not make a mistake by calling
You and me as We !

138. Nothing between us

Hey, I know its over between us.
You say we're close friends,
And I thought we were lovers,
But, we are totally strangers this time.
I thought stories might have a second chance,
To fix and heal all the things for once.
You call me up acting like you really care,
And I think that I am still in your life.
But, I can't smile now hearing you lie.
You have your roads and buildings,
Please don't try to pity on my caves.
I needed your shoulder to rest upon,
And you gave your words and went away.
Sorry that I considered you as mine,
I'm not a good person and I know it.
I don't want you to even cry on my ashes.
Hey, I know its nothing between us.
Nothing to smile and nothing to worry !

139. I wish

Wish I was beautiful,
Like that roses you admire..
Wish I would be complete,
Like just the way you desire..
Wish I had that smile,
Which you would approve..
Wish I could be that simple,
Like just the life you have ..
Wish I was a model,
Which fits in your definitions ..
Wish I could enjoy things,
Like just the way you do..
Wish I could be myself,
Atleast for once in my life..
Wish I could understand,
Love doesn't have If in it ..
Wish you could love me,
Just the way Iam ..
And Just the way I loved you !

140. Only you

Like a mother, you make me feel precious,
Like a father, you want me to be responsible.
You fought with me for some chocolates,
But, also hit that bad guy who made me cry.
You don't mock at my weakness like others do,
You make me feel strong, my big brother !
You want me to shine bright in my life,
And don't want me to repeat your mistakes.
You see yourself in my face, but seek perfection,
I have the same rules ,but they're different.
I'll shine someday but it'll take sometime.
Iam a lot clumsy, and I'm on to make it tidy.
Give me some time and I'll never let you down .
We have same genetics and chromosomes,
But, we've got different colors and opinions.
Deep inside we have the same care and love.
Brother, let me tell you for one more time,
You'll be always the reason to stop my tears.

141. We - Then and now

We were close one time,
Never leaving each other's side,
And everyone said that,
We were made for each other.
We had unmatched opinions,
Yet we smiled always together.
Never we had a thought,
That we could get away,
By the same love we had between .
We were like rain and the cloud,
You were Going down and kissing earth,
But, always came to my cloud back !
Love in your drops evaporated slowly,
When the summer came,
Took all the blackness from me,
You've made me a white thirsty cloud !
We are close today too,
You are in my heart and ,
I hope I will be in your's !

142. Keeping close

I know it's hard to keep me close,
I'm always switching my opinions.
But, I want someone to be with me ,
And make me feel safe in their heart.
Like rains send the burning sun away,
Their love should get my pain away.
I was good and earning bad names,
I was helping others but, always left alone.
There's no one now sitting on my side,
Knocking my heart door to see it,
But, always tell me to shut even windows,
You know it's hard to keep them close ,

143. Everyone's good in my life.

Everyone's good in my life,

They make me smile sometimes,

Were holding my hand sometime,

Left me alone sometimes,

Everyone's got their lives,

And nobody cares to be mine !

They say that I'm comfy,

And say they love me truly.

But when my head goes numb,

And I close my eyes,

I remember nobody this time !

They say we all are flowers,

And we all eat the same mud.

But they sing always that,

Some of us just got thorns !

Everyone's good in my life,

Until I consider them to be mine.

They need me to love and care,

But when I want to breathe,

Nobody wants me to open the window !

Everyone's good in my life,

And I'm good in their lives, after I die !

144. Can you remember?

Late in the mid night,
You came in black sweater,
Can you remember ,
How your eyes shined like ?
You sat on a wall and,
Calling your love and crush,
Can you remember,
How your voice healed me ?
You came to me one day,
In your same checkered t-shirt,
Showing Love and hate,
Can you remember ,
You didn't liked my smile !
On that and this day often,
Whenever I was down,
I slept in your lap,
Can you remember,
I said my heart loves to do it ?
From the start and ending,
The lines I'm writing,
Can you remember ,
You remained same all in them ?

ENGLISH QUOTES

145. ALL QUOTES

1)

My silence doesn't mean that
I don't want to talk to you .
I don't have words to express,
Or you don't have time to hear !

(2)

Lover (Noun) :
Person who sees you different from rest of the world, where you can be
always yourself with them, and you can tell each other that "You are mine
forever" .

(3)

This world is beautiful. Make it so for everyone !

(4)

"Yes, there are 7.8 billion people on this earth".
"But, you loose trust on everyone else,
if the person whom you have loved the most didn't made up to your heart
! "

(5)

"My children should learn everything. I should teach them all".
"My children should learn everything. I should let them to do their things
by their own".

Both are good parents !

(6)

Friends and family will help in stretching your wings. They'll not cut
them and make you bleed!

(7)

Departure hurts. But,
Departure without a good bye hurts even more !

(8)

Often, People mistake rare ones as abnormal
And, pebbles as precious !

(9)

Sometimes, its okay to see
near and dear ones become strangers !

(10)

Good parents and best friends don't avoid conversations !

(11)

Some stay close to go away,
Some go away to stay close !

(12)

Best friends are best psychologists !

(13)

You don't have to ask true friends to stay.
Because they will never go away !

(14)

Someone asked ..
"Why don't you love someone again ?"
I said
" I don't want to be a bad person again !".

(15)

Every wilted flower was Beautiful yesterday ! Likewise, Every broken

Relationship was blissful at first !

(16)

When God gives you utter darkness,
He gives you a Shining Moon also .

(17)

Understanding or not, Supporting or not,
Good friends Stay by you always .

(18)

Sometimes ,you can't but you want to and you can but you don't want !

(19)

To know ,Explore, understand & Strengthen yourself,
To support your tears all by yourself,
To be self sustaining,
Being alone is sure a positive thing sometimes !

(20)

People are like Flowers. Don't expect that flowers would be always sticked
to the tree!

(21)

When it's easy to leave
and Complex to Understand,
It's meaningless .

(22)

Life is too short to keep on searching for happiness.
Life is too long to be sad ,lingering over emotions from Past.

(23)

People who attempt suicide are not cowards. They got fed up with this
world.

(24)

When you Consider yourself "Answerable" to someone, you are valuing the relation .

(25)

She told me

"Turn into a stone in desert & butterfly in a garden "

She is my best friend !

(26)

Education is to understand things.

For understanding persons, all that you need is "Love" !

(27)

Sometimes,

The heart you loved the most

becomes the reason to hate the world !

(28)

Not in peaks & lows, my heart wants to stay flat, but not dead !

(29)

One reason is enough to love.

For leaving, it takes many !

(30)

"Sun goes, and my shadow ..

Moon goes, and my dreams ..

Wind sweeps in and out,

Sky and the air stay all the time ! "

(31)

Broken things can be fixed.

But ,cracks still appear !

(32)

A happier life doesn't need completeness,

All it needs is Satisfaction !

(33)

Discrimination is the seed for Stigma .

(34)

Ninety nine haters may cry ,

but One best friend would be enough, happy to see my smile .

(35)

Not by blood ,

Best friends are related by Heart .

(36)

Left eye : "He is bad"

Right eye : " He was good & caring once"

Heart : "your soul once found him for sharing life."

Brain :"remember good things & forget bad ones "

My tears: "do you want me some more ?"

(37)

Cloud that rains with no Thunder ,

And kids who cry hiding words under,

Are those ,who are most Unvalued.

(38)

One knows everything ,if one knows who's Who !

(39)

If emotions make us weak ,

Truths should Strengthen us !

(40)

There's a lot difference between giving reasons to "let them go " & "

keeping them hold" .

(41)

Best friend (Noun) :

That candle which lets you to step forward in utter darkness.

(42)

When you realise good deeds doesn't reflect good endings every time ,

You are now Grown up !

(43)

At the end , all that needed is only

a heart to rest upon .

(44)

Sometimes ,

Losing ability to hate,

Heart loses ability to love .

(45)

They grew up from

"The world has no place for this heart "

To

"This heart has no place for the world"

(47)

They say what you did to them

Not what you did for them !

(48)

Don't blame Road if you fell down. And don't blame situations if you fail.

(49)

Hope and Trust are like Better and Best !

(50)

When you feel there's nobody around to understand you, it's time to judge yourself!

(51)

Everyone are good, until expectations come into the scene .

(52)

When someone shares their happiness with you, You are special to them .

When someone shares their tears with you ,you are precious to them !

(53)

Exception (Noun) :

The only thing which is universal .

(54)

Once if your heart gets broken by someone, for the next time

You'll be heartless or habituated !

(55)

" You cannot leave some relations completely and you cannot be

wholeheartedly a part of them , once your heart gets broken "

(56)

The path may be difficult. But, love makes it possible .

(57)

Don't worry !

If you give ,

You'd get .

It will be balanced .

(58)

Just as framing a quote needs

careful adjustment of Words,

So does a relationship needs

careful adjustment of "Emotions" ..

(59)

Words (Noun) :

The vehicles which carry one's emotions and feelings .

(60)

Words (Noun) :

The greatest uncontrolled weapons which can make or break the things.

(61)

Better Explanations Need

Better experiences !

(62)

If facts appear Bitter ,

So does the Fate !

(63)

Be Above Threshold and within limits for sustenance.

(64)

Who loves you the most ?

"Your Tears" my heart replied .

(65)

Not only in complying ,

Love lies in defying also !

(66)

Butterfly with open wings &

Humans with open heart

Look very beautiful !

(67)

Failure is that ,

When you regret your own choice !

(68)
Without facing floods and draughts , you cannot explain what growing up actually is !

(69)
Not every tommorow is today .
Change is Inevitable .change as change
does or change the change !

(70)
People are not selfish ,
They have their own lives !

(71)
Some words Hurt,
Some words Soothe .
Some memories kill,
Some Make you alive .
Know the difference
And just Let them Go :)

(72)
Destruction (Noun) :
A process needed sometimes
for Reconstruction .

(73)
Words Hurt. But,
Memories kill !

(74)
Children are stars .
They are cute & small,
Fascinating with their
Illuminating Smiles !

(75)

Looking for Tides of Yesterday in today's ocean is just like my tears craving
for your love now.

(76)

Height of the Mountain is not
Appreciated until You get near to it.
And ,
Value of person is not known ,
Until you lose that person .

(77)

Divided or United,
A Bridge or a Relationship..
It depends upon,
How you See !

(78)

The world outside is not small. But
The window you are looking through is!

(79)

Most hardest thing in love ?
"Letting them go"

(80)

Everyone has got wings of their own.
Don't try to mess them with Your's.
Flying is a matter of Togetherness ,
And so is "Living" .

(81)

The same pen..

Writes happiest things &
Most Painful too..
First comes from heart..
Latter from Tears .
(82)
Night (Noun) :
It says, Until Sunshine I'll be..
It's not that Iam Dark, But
you can Still have your Dreams Alive !
(83)
You have fell to get up..
Not to fall Again..
(84)
Hope : (Noun)
A thing which keeps Tomorrow
Alive and Kills Today .
(85)
In this Era..
It's good to be
BAD sometimes !
(86)
Give some time to Time..
So that ..
it would heal you by time !
(87)
Greatest Medicine in world ?
The "TIME"
Because it heals everything !

(88)

Meanwhile, my day passes..
Thinking loving you
Was Difficult or
Leaving you was !

(89)

When you live as you are..
More simple the life ,
More it is beautiful.

(90)

Rain,Rainbow,Cuckoo..
Spring ,Flowers & Butterflies..
And many beautiful things in world..
Apart from You & Your love ..
But , I feel ..
Your love makes them much
"BEAUTIFUL" !

(91)

Closing eyes in darkness
Would make it more dark.
Hiding Fear in you,
Would more kill you.
Lighten the candle,
Ignite the soldier in You,
Fight against Fear !
That's all is life..
MY DEAR !

(92)

Not only Possibilities,

Know the Limitations too !

(93)

Just as, soothing Music makes

tiring journeys pleasant ,

So does a best friend

makes our life beautiful !

(94)

It definitely Hurts,

When you give much importance

to others than to yourself.

(95)

Not all Dreams come True &

Not all Truths are dreamt !

(96)

Life is not what you think..

It is what that makes you to think..

(97)

Emotions are Fragile ,

Handle with Care .

(98)

Love is where,

cure lies in pain